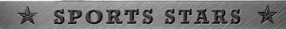

★ SPORTS STARS ★

LISA LESLIE
QUEEN OF THE COURT

BY MARK STEWART

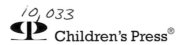

Children's Press®

A Division of Grolier Publishing
New York London Hong Kong Sydney
Danbury, Connecticut

Photo Credits
Photographs ©: Allsport USA: 33, 45 left (Al Bello), 15, 21 (Tony Duffy), 25, 29, 44 right (Otto Greule), 39 (Jed Jacobsohn), 38 inset (Rick Stewart); AP/Wide World Photos: 34, 37, 43; NBA Photos: 42 left (Andrew D. Bernstein), 38 (Scott Cunningham); Sports Illustrated Picture Collection: 10, 13, 17, 22, 26, 44 left (Peter Read Miller); SportsChrome East/West: 14 (Brian Drake), cover, 30, 35 (Rich Kane); WNBA Enterprises, LLC: 41, 47 (Andrew D. Bernstein), 3, 45 right (Greg Foster), 46 (Barry Gossage), 6 (Andy Hayt), 11 (Fernando Medina), 19 (Sandy Tenuto), 42 right (Noren Trotman).

Visit Children's Press on the Internet at:
http://publishing.grolier.com

Library of Congress Cataloging-in-Publication Data

Stewart, Mark.
    Lisa Leslie: queen of the court / by Mark Stewart.
        p. cm. — (Sports stars)
        Summary: A biography of the player who led the 1996 women's Olympic basketball team to win the gold medal for the United States.
        ISBN: 0-516-20585-4 (lib. bdg.)   0-516-26118-5 (pbk.)
        1. Leslie, Lisa, 1972– —Juvenile literature. 2. Women basketball players—United States—Biography—Juvenile literature. [1. Leslie, Lisa, 1972– . 2. Basketball players. 3. Women—Biography 4. Afro-Americans—Biography.] I. Title. II. Series.
GV884.L47S84   1997
796.323'092
[B]-dc21   96-40435
                                                                CIP
                                                                 AC

CONTENTS

★ 1 ★

GIVE THE BALL TO LISA

Lisa Leslie, the 6′ 5″ center for the Los Angeles Sparks, waits patiently as her team sets up the offense. Lisa's teammate dribbles outside of the swarming defense and prepares to pass. Planting her body, Lisa muscles aside an opponent and frees herself in the foul lane. Her teammate notices the opening. With a lightning-fast bounce pass, she slips the ball to Lisa. Before the defense can recover, Lisa gracefully spins around and banks the ball off the glass and into the basket. Unfortunately for the other team, Lisa excels at defense as well as offense. At the other end of the court, she gathers in rebounds, denies her opponents the ball, and stops any drive to the basket.

Since she first picked up a basketball in middle school, Lisa has used her tremendous size and athletic ability to dominate the sport at every level. In high school, she emerged as the top female basketball player in the country. In 1996, she led the United States women's basketball team to a gold medal at the Summer Olympics in Atlanta. Since then, Lisa has dedicated herself to her greatest challenge: using her ability and talent to ensure the success of professional women's basketball in North America.

$\star$ **2** $\star$

GROWING UP

Lisa Leslie was just four years old when she learned shattering news. Her father was no longer a part of the family. He had walked out on Lisa and her sisters, Dionne and Tiffany. Lisa saw him only once over the next eight years. From time to time, he helped out with a few dollars. When Lisa was twelve, he died, leaving the Leslies completely on their own.

Lisa's mother took action. Christine Leslie knew that she could not support her girls unless she got a better job. She scraped up the money to buy an eighteen-wheel tractor trailer and went into business for herself as a trucker.

Lisa (right) poses with her mom and two sisters in their eighteen-wheel truck.

Unfortunately, hauling loads on the nation's highways meant that Christine was usually away from her home in Inglewood, California. So she hired a live-in housekeeper to watch over the kids. "There were some sad times," Lisa remembers. "Mom had to travel so far and so long. But we understood she had to do it. It made me mature really fast. I had so much to do."

Lisa missed her mother terribly. She looked forward to the summers, when school let out and she and Tiffany traveled with their mom on those long runs. To save money, they bunked together on a narrow bed in the back of the truck's cab. It was a tight squeeze, considering Lisa had grown to 6 feet tall by the seventh grade!

Needless to say, Lisa's height attracted plenty of attention. People constantly asked her if she played basketball. It was a fair question, of course, but it became very annoying when she had to answer it over and over again. As a result, Lisa began to hate basketball. She would

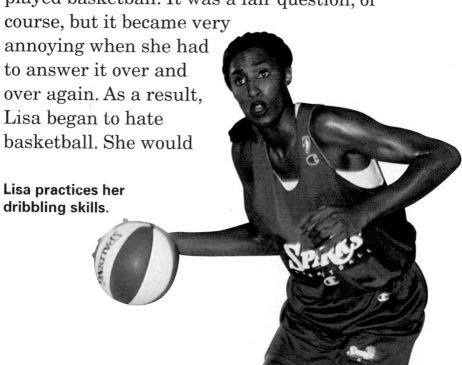

Lisa practices her dribbling skills.

have given up the game altogether had it not been for her friend, Sharon Hargrove. Sharon was a great basketball player who went on to play at the University of Nevada in Las Vegas. She talked Lisa into trying out for the junior high school team. To her surprise, Lisa found that she really enjoyed the game. "I played center for the first time," she recalls. "Our team went 7–0. I just changed my whole attitude. I guess it was my destiny, but I never knew it."

Lisa quickly learned how to use her height to dominate smaller opponents. But she knew that she could not rely on her size alone to succeed. Working with her cousin, Craig, she developed a number of shots. Lisa practiced her open-court moves, as well as her post-up game. Her goal was to become an unstoppable scorer and a tough defender. She did push-ups and sit-ups to increase her strength. She spent endless hours in hot playgrounds improving her game against the best players in her neighborhood.

Lisa developed an ability to shoot the ball from all parts of the court.

Lisa idolized James Worthy of the Los Angeles Lakers.

Lisa wanted to pattern her game after her favorite player, James Worthy of the Los Angeles Lakers. "I loved to watch James because he was a go-to player," she says. "Whenever the Lakers needed a basket in a big game, they would give it to 'Big Game James.' When I'd watch him, I'd say, 'One day I want to be that kind of player.'"

By the time Lisa enrolled at Morningside High School, she stood 6' 2½". She made the varsity basketball team easily and started every game as a freshman. Within two years, she had developed into one of the best players in the Los Angeles area. That made her mother proud. What made her even prouder was that Lisa was a wonderful student who racked up As almost as easily as she made turnaround jumpers. When she was not playing basketball, she stayed busy as the star of the Morningside volleyball and track squads. She won championships in the high jump and triple jump. Lisa was also one of her school's most popular girls—she was voted class president in her sophomore, junior, and senior years!

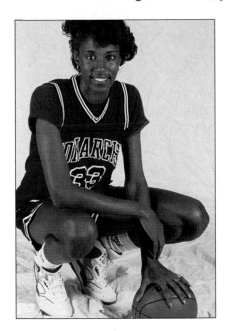

At the start of Lisa's senior season, she was at the top of every college recruiting list in the country. She had reached her full height of 6′ 5″, yet possessed the smooth scoring touch of a shorter player. The Morningside

In high school, Lisa became a star on the Morningside Lady Monarchs basketball team.

Lady Monarchs were unstoppable, dominating opponents so completely that Coach Frank Scott often pulled Lisa out of games at halftime so that her teammates could get a chance to play. Still, Lisa averaged 27.3 points and 15.1 rebounds, and she usually blocked five to ten shots a game.

In the final contest of the 1989–90 season, Lisa was the central figure in one of the most incredible games in basketball history. It was a tradition with Coach Scott to let his top senior try to break the school scoring record at the end of each year. He instructed Lisa's teammates to feed her the ball whenever she was open during Morningside's game with South Torrance High. In the first quarter, she scored 49 points. In the second quarter, she burned South Torrance for 52 more. It was only halftime, yet the Lady Monarchs were ahead 102-24 and Lisa needed just five more points to break the national high school record, which had been set by Cheryl Miller of Riverside Poly in 1982.

Lisa frequently dominated her opponents. In the background, the scoreboard shows that the score is already 83–31.

In the South Torrance locker room, the team took a vote and decided they did not wish to be humiliated anymore. Two players had already fouled out and another had been injured trying to stop Lisa. The coach came out for the second half and informed officials that he was forfeiting the game. "That was probably the highlight of my career," Lisa says. "I just started making all these baskets . . . the other team just decided not to come out to finish the game." It seemed terribly unfair that Lisa would lose her chance to make history. The referees agreed, and they awarded Morningside four technical fouls. Lisa stepped to the line and hit all four free throws to tie Miller's record. These points were later disallowed by conference officials, who pointed out that the game was officially over when the other team forfeited. Still, in 16 minutes, Lisa had played brilliantly. She took 56 shots and hit 37; she also made 27 free throws.

★ ★ ★

Lisa's 101-point performance in high school made her a target for some coaches, fans, and sportswriters. They claimed that playing so hard against smaller, weaker opponents showed poor sportsmanship. Lisa handled the controversy with maturity, especially for someone so young. She was sorry that she had made her opponents look bad but claimed it was all in the spirit of competition. "It wasn't personal. They knew I was going for the record. I thought knowing that

would take some of the hurt away from being beaten so badly. I wasn't trying to rub anybody's nose in the dirt. I was only trying for the record."

Though a pro now, Lisa still considers the game against South Torrance the highlight of her career.

3

COLLEGE YEARS

Lisa Leslie could have attended any college in the country, but she accepted a scholarship from the University of Southern California so she could remain close to home. She could hardly wait to take on the college game. Although she was careful not to seem cocky or overconfident, deep down she believed that she could become the top player in the country. After her first game as a freshman, a lot of people were beginning to think the same thing. Lisa led the USC Women of Troy against the University of Texas. She scored 30 points, hauled down 20 rebounds, got 4 steals, and blocked a pair of shots in an 88–77 victory. Lisa finished her first season leading all college freshmen in scoring and rebounding.

Lisa stretches before a game.

Lisa is one of the few female basketball players who can dunk.

That summer, Lisa traveled to England as a member of the U.S. women's team at the World University Games. No one could take their eyes off the sleek young center, especially after she surprised the crowd with a thunderous slam dunk before the team's gold-medal win against Spain. "I've been able to dunk since I was in the ninth grade because of a technique I learned doing the high jump in track," Lisa says. "I did most of my dunking during pep rallies in high school and warm-ups in college. It's more dangerous for women because other women aren't used to being dunked on, so sometimes they accidentally undercut you."

To most fans, it seemed as if Lisa had little room for improvement. But she knew better. Despite her tremendous athletic ability, she had weaknesses that opponents could exploit. She vowed to become more tenacious on defense, and she worked at establishing position closer to the basket on offense. The hours of practice paid off. Lisa's shooting percentage jumped to .550 during her second season, and she averaged more blocks per game than anyone in the conference.

She was honored as a second-team All-American, and was the only sophomore selected as a semifinalist for the Naismith Player of the Year award. Lisa continued her dominance as a junior, especially on the defensive end, where she broke the school record for blocked shots. But it was as a senior that she truly came into her own.

Lisa (right) fights for a better position under the basket.

Lisa's accurate shooting helped her reach third on the all-time scoring list at USC.

She saved her best efforts for the biggest games, especially those against conference rivals. In three wins over Stanford, Washington, and Washington State, Lisa collected 90 points and 48 rebounds.

She carried her team all the way to the quarterfinals of the NCAA Tournament before losing to Louisiana Tech. She ended her college career third on USC's all-time scoring list, fourth in rebounding, and first in blocked shots. Lisa's performance was so impressive that she was the unanimous choice as the nation's player of the year.

★ 4 ★

GOLD-MEDAL
PERFORMANCE

Lisa Leslie's basketball travels were just beginning. After her outstanding senior year, she joined the United States team for the 1994 Goodwill Games in Atlanta. She was the best player on the court, averaging 19.0 points per game and hitting more than 70 percent of her shots. Her performance helped the U.S. team win the gold medal. From there, Lisa went to Italy, where she became an immediate star in the women's pro league. At the time, there were no professional teams in the United States, so in order to cash in on her skills, she had to go overseas. Lisa remembers the experience as "learning another language, eating someone else's food, and watching television I didn't really understand."

In 1995, Lisa was invited to try out for the U.S. women's basketball team that would play for the gold medal at the 1996 Olympics in Atlanta. In 1992, Lisa had been the youngest player at the Olympic trials and was one of the final players cut. Ever since then, it had been her dream to make the '96 squad. Coach Tara VanDerveer's plan was to take her team on a year-long, world-wide tour. The U.S. team would need to develop teamwork and gain experience to beat the best international teams in Atlanta. She was asking for a huge commitment, but it was one that Lisa was ready and willing to make.

U.S. Olympic team coach Tara VanDerveer

Lisa made many close friends on the Olympic team.

"I was so excited," Lisa remembers. "There were about 56 women trying out for the team. It got cut down to 20 and I was one of them. Then we each had to go into a room where they would tell you if you made it. I went in and they said, 'Lisa, congratulations.' I just shouted 'Yeah!'"

In the 14 months prior to the Olympics, Lisa and her teammates traveled 102,245 miles (170,408 kilometers). They found themselves on courts in Russia, China, and Australia. They played some terrific teams under some very difficult circumstances, yet somehow they always managed to come out on top. When the tour was completed, their record stood at a perfect 52–0. During that time, the players really came together as a team. Lisa says it was one of the closest groups with which she has ever been associated.

By the time the 1996 Summer Olympic Games in Atlanta began, the U.S. women's basketball team was the toast of the sports world. With the men's "Dream Team" an overwhelming favorite to win the gold medal, the eyes of the basketball world turned to Lisa and her teammates. The American women had been humiliated by the Unified Team in Barcelona, Spain, during the 1992 Olympics. They had also fallen to Brazil at the 1994 World Championships in Sydney, Australia. In 1996, they expected to face stiff challenges from these opponents and powerhouse squads from China and Australia. They may have been the "home team" in Atlanta, but that guaranteed nothing if they could not play well under pressure.

Lisa grabs a rebound against Australia.

Lisa battles for the ball against Ukraine's Lyudmila Nazarenko.

The U.S. team was determined from the beginning to win the gold medal.

From the opening tip-off of their first games, Lisa and her teammates sensed that something special was happening. Regardless of their opponents, the U.S. team played brilliantly. They won their first five games easily, and Lisa established herself as the team's top inside threat in victories over Cuba, Ukraine, Zaire, Australia, and South Korea. In the semifinals, Lisa lit up the Japanese team for 35 points, the most ever scored by an American woman in the Olympics.

In the gold medal game against Brazil, Lisa's coach asked her to move away from the basket and shoot from 10 to 15 feet. The idea was to draw Brazilian center Marta de Souza Sobral away from the basket to open up the lane for quick cuts and easy follow-up shots. The plan worked on offense, but on defense, Lisa was letting her counterpart get inside position far too easily. Suddenly, Coach VanDerveer pulled Lisa from the game!

It turned out to be just the wake-up call Lisa needed. When she returned to the floor, Lisa dominated at both ends. She made 12 of 14 shots and scored a total of 29 points. The U.S. team pulled away in the second half for an impressive 111-87 win. After all those games and all those miles, they had played their very best when it counted the most, scoring more points than any

At first, Lisa struggled against Brazil.

Lisa and her teammates celebrate their victory over Brazil.

team in Olympic history. Lisa and her teammates were holding hands and had tears streaming down their faces when they mounted the stand to accept their gold medals. They knew how important their performance was—not just for themselves and their country, but for the sport of women's basketball. "It was just very emotional for me," Lisa remembers.

The U.S. team rejoices on the medal stand while receiving their gold medals.

★ 5 ★

PROFESSIONAL PIONEER

Some people would say that when you have been recognized as the country's top high school and college player—and won a gold medal at the Olympics—there is not much left to accomplish. Lisa would disagree. She believes the future is full of opportunities and adventures. "I love the game and am thrilled to have had the opportunity to play for the national team the last couple of years," she says. "If I could make a career out of this, that would be my dream. I hope that's the way things work out."

In January 1997, Lisa's dream to play professional basketball in the United States became a reality. She joined the Los Angeles Sparks, one of eight teams in the new Women's

Even with the joy and accomplishment of a gold-medal victory, Lisa insists that the future will be brighter.

Lisa receives a congratulatory kiss from her mother after being drafted by the Los Angeles Sparks.

Lisa (left) and Rebecca Lobo (right) are the two biggest stars in the Women's National Basketball Association.

National Basketball Association. As a representative for the league, she hopes to become a person young people, not just her opponents, look up to. Lisa knows that she can have a huge impact playing professional basketball and being a good role model: "Now little girls can take their balls and videotapes out and tape our games and work on their games. Ten or fifteen years from now, you will hear them saying who their favorite players were and it'll be probably one of us."

Lisa hopes to become an inspiration to the next generation of basketball players.

C ★ H ★ R ★ O ★ N

1972 • July 7: Lisa is born.

1989 • Lisa plays on the the USA Junior World Championship team, and leads the team in scoring and rebounding.

1990 • Lisa scores 101 points in a half against South Torrance High School during her senior year at Morningside High.

1991 • Lisa is named national NCAA Freshman of the Year and PAC-10 Freshman of the Year after her first season at the University of Southern California.

1992 • Lisa earns All-American honors for the first time.

1993 • Lisa is honored as the USA Basketball Female Athlete of the Year and as College Player of the Year.

O ★ L ★ O ★ G ★ Y

1994–95 • Lisa travels to Italy and plays professional basketball.

1995 • Lisa makes the U.S. Olympic women's basketball team and embarks on a 52-game world tour.

1996 • Playing before the home crowd in Atlanta, Lisa leads the U.S. team to an Olympic gold medal.

1997 • January 22: Lisa signs with the Los Angeles Sparks, one of the first teams in the Women's National Basketball Association (WNBA).

• June 21: The WNBA begins its first season. Lisa gets 16 points and 14 rebounds against the New York Liberty in the league opener.

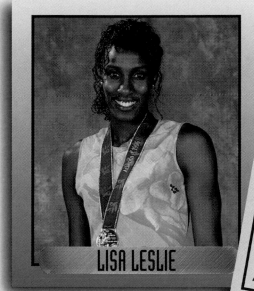

LISA LESLIE

Name **Lisa Leslie**

Born **July 7, 1972**

Height **6' 5"**

Weight **170 lbs.**

Uniform Number **9**

College **University of Southern California**

Pro Team **Los Angeles Sparks**

Honors **PAC 10 record in scoring, rebounds, and blocks; National Player of the Year (1994); All American (1993, 1994)**

LISA LESLIE

⋆ CAREER HIGHLIGHTS ⋆

- Lisa played 60 games in 1995–96, including 8 in the Olympics and 49 on the U.S. team's world tour.

- On the U.S. team's world tour, Lisa led the team in scoring by averaging 17.4 points per game.

- At the 1996 Olympics, Lisa's 19.5 scoring average ranked third behind Yamilet Martinez of Cuba (20.5) and Russia's Yelena Baranova (20.3).

★ ★ ★

ABOUT THE AUTHOR

Mark Stewart grew up in New York City in the 1960s and 1970s—when the Mets, Jets, and Knicks all had championship teams. As a child, Mark read everything about sports he could lay his hands on. Today, he is one of the busiest sportswriters around. Since 1990, he has written close to 500 sports stories for kids, including profiles on more than 200 athletes, past and present. A graduate of Duke University, Mark served as senior editor of *Racquet,* a national tennis magazine, and was managing editor of *Super News*, a sporting goods industry newspaper. He is the author of Grolier's All-Pro Biography series and eight titles in the Children's Press Sports Stars series.